THE HARRY POEMS

A CYCLE OF POEMS

By Michael L. Newell

ACKNOWLEDGEMENTS

Many of these poems (sometimes in a different form) have previously appeared in the following periodicals, to whose editors grateful acknowledgement is made: *Bellowing Ark*; *Culture Counter*; *Jerry Jazz Musician*; *Lilliput Review*; *The Long Islander*; *Lucid Moon*; *The Plastic Tower*; *Rise Up Review*; *Riverrun*; *Ship of Fools*; *Tucumcari Literary Review*; *Verse-Virtual*.

I would like to tip my cap to the following editors who have treated my work kindly over the years and been most supportive in other ways as well: Robert R. Ward, Jerry Austin, Phil Wagner, Jack Hart, Don Wentworth, Firestone Feinberg, and Joe Maita.

I would also like to thank the following folk for their kindness to my work over a span of many years and for their generous friendship: David Ellenstein, Robert Fox, Joseph Glaser, Michael Minassian, Lawrence Noel, and Ed Ruzicka.

Cover Drawing: *Harry* **by Michael Citrino.**
Author Photo: Wendy Keller.

ISBN: 978-81-8253-832-0
Tel: +(91) 9415091004 E-mail: info@cyberwit.net

Table of Contents

Table of Contents (page two)

Table of Contents (page three)

This book of poems is dedicated to the following people who have supported this project in ways that have given me permission to try something different from my usual work: the late Benjamin Saltman, the first person to read many of these poems and to encourage me to continue to explore this character; Anna and Michael Citrino who have supported my efforts as a poet for decades; Robert Wexelblatt who has been nothing but generous with his time and insightful with his comments; Stellasue Lee who has been gracious and supportive at all times and has made me feel Harry is worth knowing. I owe them all a heartfelt thank you.

"The blackbird whirled in the autumn winds.
  It was a small part of the pantomime."
Wallace Stevens ("Thirteen Ways of Looking at a Blackbird")

"The dead
  tuck their hands in our pockets..."
Benjamin Saltman ("The Sun Takes Us Away")

"We make out meek adjustments..."
Hart Crane ("Chaplinesque")

THE HARRY POEMS

A cycle of poems by

Michael L. Newell

HARRY DISCOVERS SIGNS OF INTELLIGENT LIFE

Scuff marks, frayed
edges, things
crumpled in corners, debris
half-buried, oh yeah,

people have been
here.

HARRY AT SUNSET

The tender bloom of a spring gust
brushes my face
as I stroll through the deepening
crimson of twilight.

All the day's spite and clumsy disarray
are blown away, and I
sip the air of approaching night, appraising
its bouquet of hope, its seductive body.

HARRY AT THE PARK

Today the trees
in constant motion, you've
seen the same thing
at cocktail parties, in restaurants,
on the beach, bodies
moving to the breath
of the world, do wop,
classical, and jazz;

and all afternoon, I hung
around the park
listening to the clear
running water of eucalyptus
in full swing and sway,
imagining a tenor sax in
the hands of say, Coleman Hawkins,
jamming with the wind and leaves.

HARRY DANCES

Knees crippled by time and tendinitis;
back sending warnings, "Sciatica, sciatica!"
Yet when fiddle and banjo scamper through a tune,
first your fingers, then your toes
go diddly-bop she-bop--comes one step,

comes two, comes three, the old soft glide and stride:
you're sixteen, or something like, for a minute
or three; then you gasp to a halt, still
bobbing your head, shimmying whatever
will move. Oh Yeah! Rosin Up The Bow!

HARRY DEFINES INTIMACY

To brush a crumb off
the corner of a mouth,
to adjust a strand
of hair, to casually
tilt your head to accept
such gestures.
To think nothing of the exchange.

HARRY EXPERIENCES A REVELATION

A spider's web, light
strung from a canopy
of leaves, shimmers in wind,

and a deep-throated
humming of trees bends
his knees.

He will be dazed
for days, crazed
with unutterable hope.

HARRY IN THE LATE AFTERNOON WITH CURTAINS OPENED

Gold splashes living room rug. No
metal ever so
soundlessly eased a day's
interminable weight.

Harry smiles in his solitude
and leans his face into the warmth.

HARRY LOST IN THE RIBALD WIND

Ah, the carelessness of wind
creating love, a salad
of tossed hair and blown clothing;

the tang of imagination
dresses the whole affair,
addresses exchanged in mind
only, mine not really
mine, nor would hers be
hers, nor would we
be what the wind
so casually suggests
we are, nor are we ever
what the wind would
lead us to believe;

and yet still we follow,
one fine gust after another,
love after love, alone
with the wind
and imagination...

HARRY ON CARS

"An eight cylinder phallus," Harry said.
"That's all that thing is."
His nephew scowled, "This
is the hottest thing on wheels.
No babe my age can resist it."

"Babe?" muttered Harry. "If
you ever grow up,
you may decide you'd like
someone not still in diapers."

"You're just jealous," replied
the nephew. "You simply
can't get it
up anymore." He caressed
the hood with wax and cloth.

Harry walked away, snorting
over his shoulder, "If
I did have something left,
I sure wouldn't be waving it
around in public. And if
you're such a stud, why do you need
the smoking penis?"

HARRY ON THE HISTORY OF CIVILIZATION

"I'm damned if I'll listen,"
the rum bottle sagging between right
thumb and forefinger,
"to any fool who actually believes
anything they show on t.v."

He belched, lurched
off the porch -- "C'mere, bub;
look, right there, that split log
gutted by termites and traveled
by ants, there's your
goddamned historical imperative."

HARRY'S APARTMENT CONCERTO

The dog, shlup, shlup, laps
water from her small ceramic bowl,
snuffles through the bedroom.

A baby cries next
door, her parents
shouting in Spanish.

A toilet flushes
overhead, nearby a horn sounds,
in the distance a siren.

In the city
there is no such thing
as living alone.

HARRY ON GREED

Wanting, they laid waste
to lives. Likewise I
have wanted, do want, want

too too much. Wanting we
have stripped bare every acre
of heart and mind. Blind

with wanting, we have pillaged
the terrain of our own flesh
and soul: national this disease,

and spreading from continent
to continent -- wanting wanting
wanting to want more

and more, an incontinence
of the soul and heart.
What do you want?

A good question. What
do we want, wanton
with wanting, wanting, wanting?

HARRY ON TEARS

I grow
old, sentimental,

cheap tears
for every occasion:

the terrorist's bomb,
a young woman's grace,

a shared glass of wine,
an airport embrace.

***

A friend dies.
I nod my head

at the news,
take a bite

from my perfectly
cooked steak.

My hands are
steady, face dry.

***

Why?

HARRY THE HUNTER

Belly slopping over his belt,
hair askew, shoulders drooping,
eyes popping, Harry sits
in the center of the mall

tracking all the lovely women
in and out of stores, one
door after another,
asking himself when oh when

did I get so old, rubbing
his arthritic shoulder and
sighing in wonder at
how beautiful everything and everyone

has become in those
few years between youth
and this concrete bench
easing weight on aching knees.

HARRY'S CAFE

The wind and the rain
and the rolling fog
and the years
go tumbling by

Harry glances up
now and again
faces bloom
in the cafe window

Only to fade
into outlines in the mist
and memory reconstructs
a smile a tilt of head

A grief buried deep
in the eyes
he sighs and sips
muddy coffee tries to remember

Did he recognize any passing
has he sat here a lifetime
how did he end up here
and where oh where is the staff

ONE REASON HARRY DRINKS

Early I discovered
death is easier
oh so very much
easier than life, the fragile

flowers crushed beneath heels,
the second grade buddy
whose three year old brother
shattered beneath a truck's wheels,

his stubborn little head
reduced to a blood spot
in the parking lot where we
would come to stare, to share

Max's present grief and all
our futures; and we all
share these moments, rejoicing
not yet, it is not

my turn yet, not yet
my turn, so we turn
back to life with our feeble
embraces knowing damn well

it is our turn
each and everyone
it is our turn
life being so fragile and all.

PUNCTUAL HARRY

He is never
when he is

supposed to be
there
          or here

never where
the time urges
                  or demands

him to be
never anywhere

other than
some strange

lonely world
of the mind

we check
our watches

fume and raise
our voices

when he arrives
he shrugs   smiles

ambles along
behind us

as we rush
to the next place

a look
on his face

of vague regret--
the wind at night

through a solitary
stand of eucalyptus.

HARRY FEELS A PRIMAL URGE

Birds soar,
and my bones
rustle, restless,
in smother-
ing flesh...

HARRY ALONE IN THE NIGHT

a slow rain spreads its drowsy shadows all evening
faces appear disappear reappear in darkened corners of a room
a distant splash of tires whispers of loss time regret
all night the past drowns the silent figure at the window

HARRY WATCHES A NEIGHBOR'S WIFE

Her thighs, like sun
on ice, mesmerize

and his fingers trace
the frozen rim

of his glass
of gin

as he stares
out his window

into the glare
of sun and woman

swaying in synch
with trees;

his fingers burn
in remembrance and

his lips, chips of ice,
try to form a name.

HARRY CALLS FOR ONE MORE ROUND

The slow deep rasp
of sax, tenor, Ben Webster,

and you're once again
flesh and blood

slow dancing across the rug (shag),
turn, bend, and dip,

hip to hip, your left hand
re-inventing my spine;

the last broken note falling
far beneath my feet or hearing

and you're buried too, spilled
from the horn's bell

into the limitless hell
of memory, squeeze

that note a little longer,
gasp it gone forever.

HARRY CAUGHT IN A FREEZE-FRAME

All time
distilled

into one
raindrop

slowly spreading
across the face

of a dusty
windowpane

one late February
afternoon,

Brahms Fourth
Symphony

austere in
sympathy

a low moan
from wind

knifing through
crevices

                    and a letter
                    read   reread

                    read yet
                    again.

HARRY ON RELIGION

When my heart races
at four in the morning, a vise
clamped on my chest, sweat
pouring from me like I was
a sprinkler system, then

there are nuns inside
my knees, genuflecting,
genuflecting, and the black
spots inside my head
form rosary beads.

MORTAL HARRY

Sitting outside a restaurant, Harry
eating, burrowing
into a book (no matter

of importance); lightning
snakes across the sky; brief
pause; thunder cracks a sharp whip;

Harry flinches, stares
in sudden realization:
that fast it's over,

that fast, before
he can hear
the thunder, before

he can shape goodbye
or make an act of contrition,
that damn fast.

HARRY ALONE WITH ECHOES

Her hand, he remembers,
cupped his cheek
as though he
were fragile, a vessel

to be handled
delicately, like her
mother's vase
on the counter

sprouting roses
and perfume
to fill a room;
his cheek cradled

in her protecting hand,
sheltered in memory, the reality
long vanished, along with roses,
the delicate vase, and their vows.

HARRY'S WINTER SONG

Bare, dry: winter wind,
shattered branch.

Lean against a wall,
eyes closed,

summon an image, try,
of even one green leaf.

                                        Nothing rises to fill
                                        the void inside

                                        where not even friendship
                                        can infiltrate.

                                        Night arrives,
                                        no need to open eyes

                                        to discover light's absence.
                                        It deserted a decade ago.

HARRY ALONE IN THE AFTERNOON

In spring rain faces bloom,
breath blossoms,
and crimson petals shelter in cafe windows
ablaze with stained glass radiance.
This joy is untainted, he thinks, by need or greed.

HARRY RECITES A MODERN FABLE

"Everyone read about
the perfect couple making perfect love.

"Everyone saw the movie,
went home filled
with desire and hope.

"Our streets and bedrooms swell
with wounded sound."

Harry stumbles as he leaves the bar, hums,
"Honey in Your Hips," and laughs.
A chill late evening wind slowly rises.

DOUBTFUL HARRY

Each step
a question

each gesture
a search

each answer
doubtful and

so on
he strolls.

HARRY OUT AND ABOUT IN DECEMBER

Branches sway a slow ballet.
Eager air burnishes cheeks. Steps,
slow at first, flow faster, ever
faster through deepening blush of dawn.
Silvery park grass crackles and a jet, miles
overhead, beckons; follow this way, this way, this way.

If only freedom were so simple,
thinks Harry, hungry for flight.

HARRY IN AUTUMN

Wind scatters reluctant
leaves; neighbors gather,
burn a lifetime
of memories, lean
against oak watching

crows carouse -- smell
of smoke a bitter
incense; the wind
strums bare branches, burning
leaves crackle their percussion.

Harry lights his pipe, chortles,
deliberately adds his match
to the flames, to hell
with personal history. Only fire
can warm his lonely bones.

HARRY'S PRAYER AND BLESSING

Blessed be talon, claw, feather, fur
in fury and in peace, fragile skin, gill, lung,
breath, the rising of sap, breeze-blown seed, sperm in journey,
and all things living, gone, and to be.
Praise the concept, the strife, the extreme
difficulty of life on bended knee
and come swim the sea which engulfs us
one and all. Amen. Go and sin in peace.

HARRY VISITS HIS CHILDHOOD HOME

Leaves dance a stately minuet
to the steady rhythm
of October rain

across a porch sagging
under the weight
of years;

and, for a minute,
summers, fireflies, radios,
and two in shadows

seeking a future
bloom anew
in memory's rich loam;

then the banging of the ripped
screen door shatters the moment
and he turns away, shivering...

AT THE MALL HARRY WATCHES HIS TEENAGED
DAUGHTER AND HER BOYFRIEND

Ah, the music in a glance,
the dance in a gesture,
the forms and content
of hidden love;

they imagine themselves
unnoticed, unique, first voyagers:
discovery, discovery, discovery,
yet themselves undiscovered.

And we who know these things,
observing and chuckling, are we
immune? Are we simply audience? Why
do we grow silent and afraid?

Do we grieve?
For what?   For whom?

VISITING RIGHTS AND HARRY

Aren't the sounds
pure, Daddy, she
sighed, birds
circling through trees, water
rushing down
stream over

rocks and fallen
branches, an axe
sharp and rhythmic, its
crack a distant
echo off hills? Isn't
this perfect?

He smiled, slapped
gnats circling
near, his legs
grateful finally
to be still, thinking
next time it

was his weekend,
they'd just catch
a flick, even a chick
flick, or go shopping
at the mall, anything
but tramp tramp tramp

through forest, uphill
and down, while providing
sustenance to colonies of bugs.
Harry thought the natural
world was marvelous,
at a distance or in pictures.

HARRY THE OLD OPTIMIST

Beat, beat, beat, the decrepit engine housed
within decaying chassis of my ribs;
I splutteringly move, halt, rouse
again these old bones and cartilage
to wheel another month closer to death's ledge.

Jolting over ruts that pock the road,
I still find time to study scenery,
investigate spring's blossoms as they load
fields with violent color -- plant, bush, and tree.
A future will bloom from what I cart inside me:

compost of years -- dreams, fears, triumphs, defeats,
a rich decay from which will arise new
life exuberant as these flowers spreading sweet
profusion of hope in explosions of blue,
crimson, gold, odors of church and boudoir. Askew,

all is askew -- senses tumble, spin, float,
adrift in this cornucopia of hope.
Beauty, even now can seize me by the throat
to make me loudly cry her name in tropes
as I bump and slide down life's final slope.

A DECADE PASSES FOR HARRY

No matter the distance we travel
through place or time, we'll recall how cruel

were our betrayals, the blowtorch we turned
each upon the other -- spewing words that burned

us free from shackles to stumble in half-blind
circles through a world where there are no kind

winds, words, or water to heal the cruel burns
we inflicted. We can turn, turn, and turn

again and never find a salve to ease,
a gesture to absolve our hearts' disease.

And yet no one has meant half as much as you
(flames, pain, and all). Why? I have not a clue.

HARRY AND HIS MUTT

The dog, dear dumb brute, pads
through the apartment, checking,
rechecking its world, oblivious
to confinement, to reiteration of walls.

Harry watches, amused, superior, checks his watch,

slumps out the door, trudges
to the corner, boards
a bus, a bone-numbing, wearying,
start and stop into downtown,

and, finally, enters the office
to check and recheck invoices,
numbers, his work, colleagues' work,
the big guy's work, a reiteration
of paper, word, comma, staple,
input, printout, soft copy, hard copy,
(whose copy?), until the gray wait
for the bus back, thump, bump, and clatter,

to where the dog treks
in endless journey round
its walled universe, summoning
a slight grin from Harry, weary
Harry, so aware of the greater
world which lies just outside.

HARRY FINDS SURVIVORS

I have spent my life in search
of the perfect flowering field ringed
round by forest

only to stumble
through freshly erected parking lots
or decaying alleys in wounded cities

where oil, the blood of urban arteries,
stains walls and pavement
with its bleak graffiti.

Yet even in the most scarred streets,
a weed cracks concrete,
and an older world presents itself --

certain as the Bedouin
it will outlast intruders.

HARRY DISCUSSES GRIEF

How to measure another's grief?
A single tear carves a cheek,
leaves a lifelong furrow.
You gasp at the pain and restraint,
feel a thief to witness the moment.

Another sobs, screams, punches the air,
spins in agony -- you stare
like a driver slowing
to ogle a fatal accident.

She laughs as she describes
her ten year old son, dead
ten years in a swimming accident,
telling of his love for belly flops
and cannonballs -- her eyes
search each face to be certain
each understands how special he was.
Everyone shifts uneasily.

He hugs you tightly,
tells you his marriage
is nearly over -- you feel
in his clasp the barely
contained power of desperation. You find
no words to offer, no adequate response.

There is no epiphany here, merely grief,
our inability to comfort.

HARRY LISTENS TO MISTER PARKER PLAY

wind howls through trees round
corners shaking bushes windows eaves
lightning fractures night and all
you locked up in memory too fragile
to be handled comes tumbling out
hail batters panes a flurry
of insistent notes damn it listen
this is important people are hurting here

when the rain starts after hail subsides
and the wind eases off to casual riffs
you are floating on tears the liquid breath
of every living in pain creature in the world
and no you do not can not understand this is the fundamental
music of life too simple too complex for words
thoughts movement all you can do is listen
LISTEN until silence comes and you find yourself

more alone than ever you have been...

HARRY INSPIRED BY THE PRESERVATION HALL JAZZ BAND

rattlin' bones rattlin' bones just the cost an old man pays
dancin' round his livin' room tryin' to enjoy life alone
but full of zest ripplin' with vim vigor and hot sauce fuelin'
feet ziggin' and zaggin' the blinds closed to the outside
but inside the old guy bip bop boogies all evenin'
scat singin' to old jazz tunes feelin' in them old bones
rattle rattle rattle we still got it sing the bones as feet bounce
flip flop and fly off the wall off the ceiling off the floor
into a wild bebopalooza welcome time may be fleetin'
but this moment can last forever in its inimitable whirlin' swirl
back and forth up and down and when the old dude collapses
on his couch he is laughin' laughin' wailin' like a human trombone

CREPUSCULAR HARRY

Alone in crepuscule, an old man
stares at the last vestiges of light
deepening into night; his sadness

is the same as when he hears the final
notes of a trumpet or saxophone or piano
fade into silence, a journey almost

imperceptible until completed;
all that beauty found, thoroughly
explored, then lost to the nightfall

of memory where what is stored
ultimately fades into the silent
black depths of eternity.

HARRY TELLS HIS DAUGHTER GOODBYE

His daughter slips on the garb, mental
and emotional, of an adult, ready
to sashay freely into the wide wild world
awaiting her, and yet she hesitates;

it is a big step, one that looms without pity
before her, and old Harry, tired Harry,
ready to be alone Harry, fears for her, yet
he does not know how to allay fears, hers

or his, and awkwardly pats her shoulder
as she boards the train taking her
to a future where they will seldom see
one another; both face new futures -- she

enters the whirling swirling world
of a young adult, and he recedes into corner
bars, a living room with blinds pulled down,
and midnight arguments with himself

and whatever concoction he is imbibing;
he would give her words of wisdom, but
he has none, and if he did, she would not
hear them, not now, not on the precipice

of unfettered life; their goodbye is both
tentative and final; she will move past it
as soon as the train leaves the station;
he will store it in memory and take it out

periodically to contemplate and worry over;
they will never again be so close and so distant.

MYTHIC HARRY SINGS A LATE NIGHT DRINKING SONG

winter is what I am drunk on
I am told

but if winter were not I would
be impaled on thorns

as I reached for flowers
not meant for man

I would look at women for all
seasons their dark braids streaming

their cornflower fields their red
waving poppies

rows of flowers alive
in the wind's caress

and wound myself upon
the protection woven round all beauty

or perhaps the night
would blind me

as I luxuriated in
its silken lure

why not winter as a draught
to drink deeply

it can not harm worse
than other beverages I might imbibe

so I sing of snow and ice
and winds which freeze the blood

who dares deny me
my skin grows thick white hair

I move on four legs
as well as two

I break the ice to fish
I can smell a storm

from miles away
I know shelter when it's needed

I have enough I sing the winter
I drink its melted snow

HARRY ON EATING FRESH FRUIT

Juice and sweet delicate flesh
rolled slowly round the tongue
transport me to when I was young,
when desire and hope were fresh.

Now that desire resides in memory alone
and hope is mere antidote for grief,
each savored bite becomes the act of a thief;
each swallow releases a forgotten moan.

HARRY HAS 2:00 AM FELLINI DREAMS

Stars frost the sky. Waist-deep
in snow, I stand, singing.

Crows nest in my hair: a bear
family crawls into the cave

of my stomach to hibernate;
snakes crawl in and out my mouth.

Hidden high in a tree, a woman
laughs and laughs.

Frenetic, a little man yells, "Don't
think, do," every time I ask a question.

Trying to wake up, I discover
I'm trapped in a VCR.

HARRY REMEMBERS

That old plant your mother gave you
that you left behind and I never
liked all that much

just sprawled along the sink ledge
like some old basset hound
trying to sleep -- or die.

The first couple of weeks I watered it
daily. Gradually
it was ignored.

When looked at again, its soil
was dry as shale; and water after the fact
never revives much of anything,

a fact we relearned yesterday
talking on the phone about
giving it another chance.

After I hung up,
I tossed the plant
into the dumpster.

Still I hung around
for a bit wondering
if my action was premature,

as I had done after you hung up,
hanging on for a minute or two,
hoping for your voice to come back on.

HARRY SEEKS A WITNESS

A chair warmly entangled
in afternoon sunlight
embraces me
as I slowly slide
into its arms,

rub my fingers lightly
over mahogany, sip
cocoa, and remember
your fingers tracing whorls
through long afternoons

spent listening to Ben Webster
and Oscar Peterson
(on sax and piano)
investigate the terrain of love
and its various disasters.

It was impossible, we thought,
for us to ever truly know
these things; I remind myself
of this as I toast the 8X10 glossy
you left behind and search for fingerprints

on chair, on cup,
on flesh, on shafts
of light warming skin;
even the cocoa, scalding hot,
is scrutinized for evidence.

HARRY SEES A GENERATION GAP

Stars sprawl across night's canvas
in casual disarray, lovely
as sway of thigh and sturdy calf
you laughingly display under a spring moon

which burnishes a path across waves and sand.
Such grandeur of gesture is easily worn
only by the reckless young
or nature itself. We who are older

fear displays of flesh and the world.
Our vision has turned inward and burns
old hopes to ash. Yet still
your laughter endows us with our past.

AGING HARRY TALKS TO HIMSELF IN THE MIRROR

Year after year, body and mind, change upon change
upon change (no matter how much, no matter how often),

I still remain the same; I alone must take all blame;
face and body that I see have been formed by me

and me alone, and yet somehow my essence has
never changed: cantankerous, willful, stubborn,

and defiant toward authority, toward convention,
toward acceptance or belief in the world's norms.

Even he who argues with me in the mirror is a nuisance.
Who are we who argue so, look similar, and never agree?

HARRY THE PHILOSOPHER AT THE CORNER BAR

I have heard
a word or two
in my life
that summed up

all the days
thrown away
in careless disarray
year upon year;

I have listened
and nodded, agreed
from time to time
how best to describe

this perpetual waste
which can be traced
through all lives
young or old;

some use the word
time or thief
or both; but
I think you spoke

best when last
night you named
all our losses
by one word, grief.

Each glass we drink,
each rough joke we
share, every burst
of senseless anger

is an attempt to find
meaning in all our
inevitable losses that
define us as human.

HARRY TAKES AN ANTHROPOMORPHIC STROLL

The leaves
of the eucalyptus

burbled in the breeze
with the sound

of a large cocktail
party where everyone

wants to be heard
but no one wants

his or her words
to be understood;

and I could have sworn
as I walked past

two or three
trees nodded

in my direction
as though offering

me a cocktail or
a word of advice.

SOLITARY HARRY

1.
dust collects
on the unsaid.

2.
shadows too intimate
for scrutiny.

3.
a sudden sound,
a single listener.

4.
a bed doubled in size.
a night without the brush of thighs.

HARRY BEARS WITNESS

1.
Her last words, threads
fluttering.

2.
Ants ruin eyes.
Weeds sprout through ribs.

3.
Wind fills weeds
and skeleton.

4.
Ants thread soil
beneath ruins
with time's runes.

HARRY ON A LAZY SUMMER DAY

After a long day of bourbon, beer, and wine,
Harry is certain he sees the world more clearly --
life is cruel, friendship is a pipe bomb waiting
to go off in your face, and a strong drink

is a man's best friend. He slips down into a lawn chair
as neighbors walk away tired of his caustic
remarks, and he realizes the sun is fading into tomorrow;
the cooling air brings him some peace, and he drifts

off to sleep, unaware of time or place; a kind neighbor
slips a blanket over him, then walks away shaking
her head; she knows Harry won't wake up until morning,
and then will be uncertain how he ended up asleep

in his front yard once again. Harry dreams of the past,
a woman and daughter who loved him, and hope, that gift
which calmed his rage at life and which he has misplaced
for oh so many years. Eventually, he snores with vigor.

HARRY ON A BENDER

all afternoon Harry rages   free jazz   his voice
as wild as Ornette Coleman's sax on "Song X"
free associative riffs   on neighbors   friends
former family   present family   politics
history   love   hate   beauty of nature   destruction
of nature   why everyone who disagrees with him
displays their ignorance   why everyone who agrees

with him is a wimp   his voice rises falls grows harsh
mellows over a beer with bourbon chaser   his brain
is a boiler room of malice toward a world he wants
to love but always gets wrong   beauty breaks his heart
tree bush river stream mountain soaring sun moon

wind rain woman young or old athletes in full stride
and startling grace   he resents his aging hulk his wispy
moustache his aching knees his fleeing hair   his voice
whispers   shouts   crackles from misuse   grows hoarse
from wild riffs that run on and on for hours at a time
until he stumbles indoors with his dying voice trailing
behind him   leaving a neighborhood grateful for silence

HARRY TAKES A WALK

My body slung across
grass, visual echo
courtesy late afternoon,
tune from the underworld;

tree and bush spread
beside me, no prejudice
here, earth and sun equal
opportunity mimics.

I imagine this dark
substanceless creature
scouting ahead my future
tunneled by worms and maggots;

even so, its heft and shape
equal in significance my own,
perhaps surpassing, I realize,
watching termites delve into wood.

HARRY IN THE STORM

Fierce gusts
rattle windows,
rain splashes against panes,
elms shudder above loose roof tiles,
he smiles.

HARRY CONSIDERS HIS PAST

A chair warmly entangled
in late afternoon sunlight
embraces me
as I slowly slide
into its arms,

rub my fingers lightly
over mahogany, sip cocoa fortified
by bourbon, and remember
your fingers tracing whorls
through long afternoons

spent listening to Ben Webster
and Oscar Peterson
(on sax and piano)
investigate the terrain of love
and its various disasters.

It was impossible, we thought,
for us to ever truly know
these things; I remind myself
of this as I toast the 8x10 glossy
you left behind and search for fingerprints

on chair, on cup,
on flesh, on shafts
of light warming skin;
even the cocoa, scalding hot,
is scrutinized for evidence.

THE DAY HARRY SAID GOODBYE

That which we shaped
and honed and lived

has withered. Dig a hole,
fill it, murmur goodbye.

Ten years from now, look
back from one of life's hills

and remember a day or an hour
when the world flamed with hope,

when we walked without need
of words, touch, or reassurance,

when shared presence was
sufficient to the moment.

What will survive, says Harry,
will be memory slowly burning to ash.

HARRY ASKS WHAT PENANCE WILL SUFFICE

You were angry.

The words spoken to you
were not to be tolerated.

You lashed back, provoked.
Tears tears tears and more tears.
Justified, you left unmoved.

Later, witnesses said the words
you heard were never
said, never, not by anyone
in the room.

They are wrong, they are wrong.
Aren't they? Are they? If not,
how will you enter
that room again, how
speak to the one you damaged? How?

Don't ask the wind for forgiveness.
Don't pray. The injury was not elsewhere.
It was here. It was today.
What words will serve you? You still
feel injured. Why? You still rage. At whom?
The return will be the longest walk you have made.

CRAZY HARRY

Harry, crazy under a midnight moon, alone
on his patio, listens to the dolor bone deep
buried in the laments of Miles Davis
playing *Sketches of Spain* with admirable mastery

of the Harmon mute, breaking and bending notes,
letting the heart wail, the mind lost in time and space,
and Harry harmonizes, his raspy voice
provoking a neighborhood dog to howl.

When lights turn on nearby, and voices shout
epithets abusing the concert of Harry and the dog,
Harry wanders inside and dives into some red wine.
He turns the music down and eventually sleeps,

tears on his cheeks, wine on his breath, and dreams
that he composes a symphony of oceanic size, all grief,
that he sings with many voices to passing dolphins as he stands
on a deserted seashore amid crashing waves and circling seabirds.

HARRY HEARS FAINT FADED MUSIC

the photo bleeds the past
faces dimmed and buildings
distant and muddied by time
your smile breaks my heart
with its tentative beauty its askew

embrace of pain anticipated
and due to arrive sooner than
even you realized and I wonder
who is that standing behind you
arms enfolding your shoulders

looking content and totally unaware
of the years to come
why does this image of you and me
and our friends and acquaintances
overwhelm my senses as though

I were listening to a blues lament
sung and played by Muddy Waters
B B King and John Lee Hooker
while jazz dancers enact love
and its inevitable loss

all those decades past
whisper their faint faded
music through photo and memory
and I would ask forgiveness
for what was and what wasn't

except I do not know the words to say
or who would listen and I lift my eyes
to a sliver of moon sailing
behind storm clouds its silvery promise
sailing away with love's abandoned cadences

HARRY ON CERTAINTY

Certainty is
what I
never have

that rock
might be
a snake

tightly curled
or someone's
rough jacket

casually dropped
or dirt
clods loosely

piled or
it might
simply be

a rock
certainty never
is what

I have
no assurance
merely possibilities

SCHIZOPHRENIC HARRY ON A LINE BY RIMBAUD

("I is another" -- Rimbaud)

Ain't we all, Jack, several anothers,
all a-bother, agape, agog, gasping
at the   the   the   sheer impertinence of all them
others to visit my mirror my face she and he
and heshe   shehe   I could get the giggles here
but this is damned serious shit man who are
all these interlopers bursting out my skin
their voices arguing out my mouth hell they can't
even agree on how to share the space properly
I'd go to court and get them evicted
but police won't visit this neighborhood and these clowns
think they're above the law they won't even pay
rent they claim squatters' rights and then complain
I don't give them enough space to live properly
YEAH I IS ANOTHER too damn many others
and it's getting hard to sleep when I can't even
find space to crash in my own bathtub...

Who are all you people anyway?

SAYS HARRY, LIFE IS A WILD FLING

In a wild dance on a ledge soaked with rain,
grief and elation lead feet to soar and return
to the slippery path that guides us through life;
tears, wailing, and wild exuberance fearlessly flung

in fate's indifferent face lift feet to dance -- perhaps
a fandango -- with any partner brave enough
to join and face life clapping hands in triple meter,
expanding and contracting along with triumph

and disaster until the eventual collapse
into nothingness awaiting us all;
and (with luck) a handful of those left behind
quietly applaud whatever fortitude the departed

have shown through their days, long or short,
caught in the dangerous dance along
the alluring ledge that has served as pathway
to help define who they are, such as they may be.

HARRY HAS A VISION

The leaves were falling when I heard the news
that a lad from my youth had passed away;
and each leaf that tumbled into yard, street,
and gutter, seemed to bear with it a rider,

each with a different face from my many years,
and each face sang a song of loss and passion
and time as an inexorable foe for even the best
and bravest and most capable of those I had known;

and the rising wind surged into a dirge as it sang
through branches and leaves with the wild
sorrow of the uilleann pipes, and I crumpled
against the wall under the weight of the leaves

and the imagined freight they carried with them,
and I stared, silent, into the deep approaching night.

HARRY'S MEMOIR

She smiled, stretched out a hand,
and he walked away;
for thirty years he's remembered

and caught glimpses of her: in supermarkets,
in snack bar lines waiting to buy popcorn,
at bus stops, in department stores,

on beaches, in airports, through rain-streaked car windows
on freeways; he's remembered
and rehearsed dialogue for a second chance.

But they never knew one another; they were
just faces passing on a campus
like wind-flung seeds or litter.

Still he repeats her possible names,
sounding them carefully as though he had
a decision to make, as though she could hear.

The wind snatches his voice, hurls it
behind him, rips involuntary tears from his eyes. He's afraid
to look over his shoulder, afraid nothing is there.

HARRY ON THE LAMP

Not its dim and questioning, its
circumscribed, its fading (or brilliant)
light, no. Its value inheres

in shadows it creates, all
of life, us them it, all
implicit in indefinable

shapes coiled on fringes
of vision where sight and night
blur into suggestion, where hope

and fear lap across each
other's shores in a merging
of seas, an erasure of beaches.

For light and darkness are not
our worlds -- we are creatures
of the dusk who sail shoals and reefs,

visit nearby islands. The vast sea
or boundless prairie, the unmediated sun
or fathomless dark, these are too pure.

We shelter in the tentative, the shifting,
the half-seen, the innuendo of lamp
spilling through the dark.

HARRY SEEKS A WAY OUT

There is the hiss and splatter of rain,
(Soaking window, screen, and bedroom floor),
And distant whistle of a freight train.

We sit and nurse our whiskey and shame,
Wonder if lies spread as airborne spores.
There is the hiss and splatter of rain.

Betrayals can be hard to explain.
It's far easier to listen for
The distant whistle of a freight train.

Our words only give us drunken pain,
Our shared lives are mold upon the floor.
There is the hiss and splatter of rain.

As accusations begin to wane,
Each thinks of escaping through the door
To distant whistle of a freight train.

It does not matter who is to blame,
Who cannot last even one night more.
There is the hiss and splatter of rain,
The distant whistle of a freight train.

HARRY ASKS A FRIEND, WHEN AM I?

Not now, I'm never now. I am about
to be, or have been, or should, could,
or might have been, would like, consider, dream,

pray, enjoy, seem to be, any tense and mood but
present indicative actual tangible shake the senses alive.
Perhaps, she said, you are caught

in the permanent subjunctive -- you know
this is a disease that could be treated.
Really, said I; were it to happen, would it

solve everything? Would I be sensual, athletic,
charming, thin, and clever? Perhaps these things
are safer in the imagination. Were they

to happen, would I know me? Would my mirror
catch up to the new me? Would my reflection
vanish in disgust or envy? Would old friends

offer congratulations or merely gossip among themselves?
Who, did you say, could treat my condition? Could
I use my Visa card? Would the government have a record?

As her car backed out the driveway,
I yelled, do I need a referral?
Can my money be refunded if I don't like the results?

Will I know the names of the day, week, month,
year, city, county, country, and job I'm in?
Will cornflakes taste like brie and milk like mead?

Will I still need to brush after every meal
and change my underwear twice a day?
Will I discover who, what, and when I am?

HARRY ON THE BETRAYALS OF SPRING

The betrayals of spring are beyond number.
Every plant, bush, tree, bird, and animal (birthed
in the promise incessantly murmured by wind, brook, and blood)
hum with the wonder and hope of life.

Wait. Wait for a short time;
hear the slowing of blood;
feel the ache of crumbling limbs, bones, and joints;
smell the decay that surrounds all things.
In our corruption we look around
to see everywhere the betrayal of life.

As leaves shimmer golden under golden sunlight
before docile surrender and drifting to dust,
as plants droop under life's weight, as faces wrinkle,
as birds fall to earth a final time and settle

in the long grasses which will soon lay brown
in brown soil, as tomorrow or the next day our words
will collapse to silence, as all smells surge and spread
into emptiness, so our love will betray itself
to the lonely wind which will itself eventually expire.
At last even betrayal will have been betrayed to nothing.

HARRY IN A CAFE LISTENS INTENTLY

Night music: a breeze
of voices, glasses clink,

waves of laughter surge,
a hush descends, even the humming

lights still; then a rising trill --
male, female, femalemale in

a memory of birdcall, spring,
and the thaw of mountain water

over jagged rocks; its disappearance
into black earth where worms murmur;

soon scraping feet summon
a future, a casket slipping

into earth and a fading scuffle
through leaves into stillness;

a lid shuts; a door
closes. Echo, echo, echo.

The world is filled
with echoes.

HARRY ON BEING SOLITARY

There is no stillness, no solitude, no silence
in the mind that compares with being alone
in a crowd where conversations are shouted
on mobile phones, where preening walkers
strut and seek envious eyes, where half-strangers

converse about a host of topics which matter
not at all to those involved in the nattering
discourse, a bubbling babble of poorly formed
thoughts, wild attention seeking gestures
which demand look look look at me,

and laughter sounds like a television laugh track.
Escape is a quiet room where one or two people
mean what they say, and listen to responses,
and words echo with a power never felt
in the wild dance of crowds afraid to be alone.

HARRY ENTERTAINS HIMSELF

Harry sits on his porch on a shaky three-legged stool,
drinks shots of tequila, talks to himself, shakes
his head in wonderment at the world passing by.

Who are all these people taking pictures of themselves
with phones, unaware of anything but themselves,
he mutters, and begins to name those passing,

gives them names not fit for polite conversation,
downs another shot of tequila, feels his head spin
so fast that he thinks everyone on the street is dancing,

stumbles to his feet, tries to do a jig, slips to one knee,
stands back up laughing; he notices rain is falling,
the streets are emptying; his spinning head dances

everyone off the street and into nearby coffee shops;
he staggers out into the rain, does a slow waltz with his cane.

HARRY'S SONG WELCOMING AUTUMN

a brilliant raiment covers the ground--
a panoply of autumn leaves

hear trees
grieve in a smoky wind

children roll upon
crackling red and gold

their own future in shattered
leaf fragments foretold

ah the bold gestures
and shouts of those unaware

of time's inexorable casual fist
squeezing shut their hearts' valves

their quintessence transformed
to dust plant tree leaf

a brilliant raiment strewn
upon an indifferent ground

SOLITARY HARRY DREAMS A HISTORY

I saw my love
in a ship of clouds,
prow to the horizon;

her hair flowed
back in waves,
sun-dazzle, sun-dazzle;

I leaped, I reached,
I grasped the air,
(who can hold the cold wind);

memory settles in the black ocean;
smoothed by water and time, it rises;
lodges in my pocket --

I stroke it, an amulet
born in the sun, shaped by water,
carved in the image of regret.

HARRY ALONE IN THE DEEPENING DUSK

in silence and stillness
he casts lines of thought
and reels in

(with difficulty)
various versions of

himself

he stitches each to each
trying to recreate a whole

but is left staring at a scarecrow
which casts shadows
in all directions

HARRY FACES OLD AGE

Amidst ruins of age
he whispers,
"Am I still here?"

HARRY ON TIME

My hair blossoms
into silvery silk, time's gift
for his many thefts.

HARRY STARES AT APPROACHING MORTALITY

All the days of all the years I have lived
echo again and again in my turbulent mind;
voices I knew and have forgotten, then rediscovered,
murmur, whisper, shout, sing, accuse, forgive, lament,

and remind me of all I have learned and misplaced in memory;
all that has stunned me with beauty and baffled me
with complexity, all that has challenged,
terrified, raised my mind and heart to unexpected
heights and depths, and then left them baffled

and named me "He who is alone, alone, ever alone,"
then granted me fear and joy, loss and wild
unnameable hope that is unquenchable as my thirst
for knowledge, friendship, and whiskey rye whiskey

wherever I may go, always looking far down the road,
seldom seeing what is found along the approaching roadside;
time is never enough, but always a blessing; those who care
bring ecstasy, yet solitary days always follow;
all seems possible, but nothing lasts, and I sing

wherever I walk, sing alone but full-throated,
knowing I have no idea when the end will come or how,
but knowing it is closer and closer, day by fading day,
and I bow to the inevitable approaching darkness.

HARRY CONSIDERS TIME

Harry tells his buddy Morty,
"In the woods, I saw
a hummingbird dart

with speed and wild
freedom, unfettered
from all restrictions

save time, inexorable time,
ruthless, unyielding time;
who am I, then, a mere plodder

to mourn my losses, when
even the swiftest and brightest
will surrender in the end?"

BIRDWATCHER HARRY

One hummingbird, then another, then
another flits past my window as they
trek to a neighbor's bird feeder,
an avian community center.

I would feel slighted, but I fully
understand that I have nothing to offer
save my applause for their brilliant flight
patterns and colors that set my mind

and heart agog, agape, awhirl in wild
surmise of what it is like to own the air.

HARRY'S SUMMATION OF A FRIEND'S LIFE

Ragged in the world, she
whirled past astonished faces
carefully tied in place,
nylons straight and vests adjusted.

She knew alleys lit by starlight
and the wind's howl on a bender;
her tangled locks and muddy teeth
testified to her griefs.

All of heaven, all of hell could swallow
Bonnie's bones and fell her days,
without dazing her will, that remarkable
growth sprouting from her every gesture.

When they came to bury her, her lips
were curled, a joyous snarl, and all
who visited at the last remembered only she
was the one never vanquished, never lonely.

She buried daughters, sons, and husbands;
lost generations of friends and lovers;
cast away church and state, created a slate
all her own on which to fashion a life's meaning.

Save your Requiems and toll no bells; what was
buried here today no grave can hold nor eulogy
enfold -- a woman's life unfolded, folded into
earth, sprouts anew through all who knew her worth.

HARRY ON WILL

Inebriated Harry in the park says,
"The censor censures any who violate
law, custom, or traditional belief;

"no one may think for self or act
without reference to judge, priest,
mother, father, or ruler."

Said the reckless sinner to his world, "I will
be what I am, where I am, when I am, and I dismiss
your contempt, your naming, your excommunication.

"If this means I am alone, I am
alone by choice, by will, by imagination,
and I deny your right to shape my path.

"Each man can choose the direction of his feet,
and his mind is freer still, and his heart unnameable."
Harry tips his hat and walks on unaccompanied.

HARRY AND THE ABANDONED OLD MAN

"I am deaf now
to nuance," he said
(the old man in the cafe's

corner seat),
"the rise and fall,
the swing and sway.

"Trees no longer
sing to me, the plants
have forgotten my name,

"and even the wind speaks
only in a monotone.
The stars, oh yes, the stars --

"they stare and offer no solace.
The years have passed by and left me,"
says he, "staring into a broken mirror."

Harry eyeballs him, mutters, "Drink up,
buddy, a little whiskey goes a long way.
It will help you reach the dawn."

Harry belches, slaps the old guy
on the back, refills their glasses,
and toasts the bar which shelters them.

HARRY CONTEMPLATES DISCARDED DREAMS

A feather floats,
glides, slides,

to earth
and is

crushed by
a care-

less foot.
How easily

obliterated,
the delicate.

How fragile are
flesh, bone, mind,

how transient
are elegance,

beauty, imagination,
wit's brief displays.

One errant step,
one miscalculation,

and dreams shatter
like autumn leaves.

HARRY'S DRUNKEN RANT ON LANGUAGE

"Split the tongue and broken
words tumble out, hyphenated
in all the wrong places, so split

the scene until thread and needle
can be found to sew up what's wrong

with the anatomy, then reconstruct --
the new linguistic model for the time --
reconstruct what has sprawled, splattered,

split, splodged, upon the floor, stoop,
hallway, courtyard, street, and alley, fragments

hidden in bushes, cellars, buried
in tree bark, fur of barking dogs and
mewling cats, reconstruct vowel, consonant,

and diphthong, bring the word to the idea, meld
lexicon and syntax, dissolve form into function,

function into meaning, meaning into a full spectrum
search for sense and sound. Reconstruct.
And watch the world's semantic cops and literary gurus

pull the stitches loose and flood the global neighborhood
with broken words, maimed thoughts, and scornful laughter."

Harry snorted laughter into his whiskey glass, then stumbled
from the bar waving his left hand behind him as though
he were slapping away all there as if they were gnats or flies.

HARRY SAYS NEVER

is never never
is never what it seems to mean
for instance Lear says

Never Never Never Never Never
yet every time the play
comes round again

Never is ever there
and so is Cordelia
and of course the old argument

did old Willy Shakes
write the words of Shakes
and some say never

and others say you never
had an argument
at least not one

which was ever
any great shakes
and so shaken and stirred

but not chilled
we twiddle de
and twiddle dum away

never finding an end to it all
whatever never
really means

HARRY AND MORTIMER AMAZED

Deep in his cups, Harry throws
an arm around the shoulders
of his long-time drinking buddy,
Mortimer, and proclaims,

"Knowledge requires
search, an excavation
of the deepest strata
we can reach.

"Wisdom arrives
with realization that knowledge
never is enough. It merely
cracks a window

"to gaze at life's meaning, revealed
as an insolvable maze."
The two nod in agreement, slap hands,
and return to staring into half-filled glasses.

HARRY ON HISTORY

"History," he mutters to his buddy,
the always patient Mortimer,
as they nurse a couple of beers
through a late afternoon,

"History fades to shadows;
a man once important
expands into myth;
eventually, only tall tales remain."

Mortimer nods his head in support
of his friend who belches
and states with the authority
of someone with too much to drink,

"Nothing is ever what it seems,
certainly not the stories handed
down to us." Twilight slowly
envelops the two philosophers.

HARRY LOST IN CREPUSCULE

Seated at his dining room table,
Harry imbibes fading pale yellow light
above tree-capped hills embracing the sky.

No drink is nearly so fine, he thinks
not brandy, rum, whiskey, or wine;
naught raises his spirit or elevates his mind

with gusto of day's metamorphosis
from pale ale to gloaming's deep
purple wine bathing all who are heedful,

afoot or indoors, with blood
that weds light to dark. Harry
takes a deep breath, exhales,

and with immense satisfaction, he slowly
unleashes a wide smile, leans his head back
into interlocked hands, and welcomes night.

A COLOR SCHEME FOR HARRY

All day his work
is gray, all day
his mouth tastes of charcoal,
all day mist hangs over eyes
of co-workers; all day all day
all day. Muzak rolls in his ears
in harmony with bus tires

on his ride home. He slumps
toward his front door, key in hand,
and notices fog seeping from his bones
to blanket the unwary neighborhood.
He sighs and rain clouds form. He stumbles
up three flights of stairs in a downpour
and slips into the shelter of his living room.

He folds himself onto a couch. He glances
around the room to find painters
have discovered where he lives
and painted his walls and ceiling gray.
His black dog whines and creeps
across the floor; she's gray. Exhausted,
he sleeps, dreams: gray gray gray...

HARRY DISCUSSES JOB SECURITY

Finagling, squirming, writhing
toward a YES, or at least
an OKAY, so some sort of permission
exists when events deteriorate, implode,
destruct into blame, leave
someone (there's always someone) holding

the bag, the unlocked barn door,
the keys to the room where
the paper was shredded, turned
to ash, scattered into the anonymous wind,
someone (in short) to take the fall,
do the time, sing MEA CULPA, but not

YOU who have the HIGH SIGN
the NOD, the thoroughly covered ass,
oh no, you'll be here for the next
soft-shoe, buck-and-wing, glide to the side
when the orchestra gets overheated
and the conductor starts looking for replacements.

HARRY ASKS HIMSELF WHO GIVES A DAMN

Sitting alone on the porch, Harry
listens to the bird in a nearby tree
scold him for intruding on
the feeding ground of the noisy creature;

being chastised by something so small
leads him to once again chastise himself
for all the things which have gone wrong
over the past month: her leaving, loss of his job,

the mess in the sink, the bills piled on the desk
in the living room artfully decorated
with fried chicken bones and boxes
of stale half-eaten pizza which serve as

ash trays for partially smoked cigarettes,
and as accompaniment to beer cans and bottles
tossed on floor, couch, chair, and window sill;
he remembers, before she left, talking about

the need for an interior decorator; well, he
has taken that task on himself; the rooms
throughout the condo certainly detail
his state of mind and heart and care for life;

form and function have come together, he thinks,
and laughs loudly enough to start the bird,
who has gone silent, back up again; he gives
the bird the one finger salute and drifts off to sleep.

HARRY IS LOST

Is that a hole in the air
where once you stood?
I thrust my hand into
the empty space, draw back

no one, nothing,
save the rustling of wind
and a sound which might
be wings beating away

from where I stand.
I shout your name. In return
not even an echo, only
the overwhelming weight

of silence where once
there were shared words,
the Morse code of gesture
and glance, the medicine

of touch and embrace. Diminished,
without looking back, I walk away.
Strewn by a crow on a pole, debris
of raucous laughter litters my path.

FOR EACH THE CROSSING AWAITS MURMURS HARRY

All of life is a-swirl, hopes hurled in every direction,
a hurricane of javelins carved from bone, heart,

and soul, flung willy-nilly wherever and however

one can unfurl oneself, until the great night approaches
and swallows all the joy, hate, love, fear, anger, desire,

dream, dread, and confusion that inform our lives,

and all that is left is hope that one will cross
Tennyson's bar sans terror sans expectation sans anything

save the measured, deeply sorrowful, elegant notes

of Handel's Sarabande charting the ocean's rise and fall
on the unknowable trip into eternity's vast reaches.

HARRY HEARS A PARLIAMENT OF CROWS COMPLAINING

Don't look up. They have commandeered
telephone wires and thick tree branches
to caw, gabble, prattle, and babble
about perceived ills of the world.
All hoarse invective that they hurl
sounds like the slurs that daily dribble
from my neighbors' lips in drunken trashing
of one another and all others who live in fear
of themselves, locked inside bottles of beer,
places where they forget all they hold dear.
Wait long enough -- their voices grow hoarse,
devoid of beauty, coarse enough for crows to endorse.

HARRY PAST MIDNIGHT

All night, every night,
I hear voices calling
from fields of childhood.

Their spectral faces obscure
the ceiling. Their words
drift in and out like a radio

on a cross-country drive;
I realize they are not calling
me; they are calling others

who have left us behind,
as they search for halcyon days
abandoned in the name of growth.

I weep to discover they are
no happier than we who are
left behind on dusty asphalt

and concrete roads that have
paved over the playing fields
of childhood. I would call

all whose spectral voices
haunt me to tell them we are
no better off than they are,

but my dry tongue swells,
and the only words that escape
my lips are my own cries for help.

HARRY AFTER MIDNIGHT

After midnight, the moon sliding behind
a bank of clouds, the streets silent, no bird,
man, cat, dog, or raccoon in sight or sound,

the house mumbles in its unique
lexicon of creaks, whispers, and groans,
a serenade barely audible that unfetters

all the losses, mistakes, foolishness, grief,
and barely contained anger buried in heart
and mind of the solitary listener who stands

by an half-opened window and mumbles
to self and night barely remembered prayers,
and welcomes sight of a meteor flashing

through night above distant tree-draped hills,
as he feels his bones clamoring to break free
from skin and take flight into eternal night.

HARRY HAS ONE OF THOSE DAYS

You show up for the event in a crisp
new three piece navy blue suit
only to find everyone in jeans or sweat pants.
You turn to the stunning brunette on your left
and tell her how you always believe in dressing up
no matter what the occasion;
she says you have a soup stain
on your tie, your socks don't match,
and -- worst of all -- your breath reeks of garlic
from the pizza you grabbed at lunch.
Before you can get it back together, your boss
pops up at your elbow, says your report is overdue,
you missed today's staff meeting, and do something
about your shoes -- they are scuffed and out of style.

When you get home, your dog growls
as you enter the living room; you discover
the roof is leaking sewage again
through the light socket over the dining room table;
and your phone has been disconnected.

You kneel to attempt some evening prayers -- any
port in a storm, right? Your back
goes out again, and your right knee locks
so you can't get back up. Just then
the doorbell rings. You eventually
manage to answer it. It's the manager shouting
your last rent check bounced.

You finally get to sleep and dream all night
of your ex-wife and her new husband.

HOPEFUL HARRY

She speaks.
His knotted

fist feathers
open -- the petals

of her
fingers

mingle with his
surmise.

Whatever she says
will surprise.

HARRY LOST

All those alleys, back lots, open
fields we raced through,

what black hole swallowed them
and when? Why didn't we notice?

Opening a window we gaze on
building upon building, rows of clenched fists;

the streets wander, lost beneath feet
seeking what has vanished.

HARRY AT HIS RICH SISTER'S BACKYARD DINNER PARTY

He spat, spat again, and yet
one time more he evacuated
all the bile he could gather
to hurl at the earth
as though purging all
disappointment, disgust, dread,
and anger, all the accumulated
detritus of living.

He rubbed his mouth raw
on his faded greatcoat, glared
at all of us as if
daring even one to raise
issues of propriety and manners.
"Can't," he snarled, "any of you
damn fools talk about anything
that doesn't revolve around money,

the neighbors, or how much better
things were thirty years ago?
Goddamnit, people, the sky's falling
and you're worried whether the servants
are stealing your pathetic silverware."
We all shuffled off, uneasy
witnesses at a car wreck,
not wanting to be called to testify.

HARRY ON PROGRESS

Footfalls haunt night; tin cans rattle
through shadows splashed
across night walls by shifting neon;

ghosts, man, ghosts
of last year and last week;
and today will be

tomorrow's ghost riding
past in an ambulance
with the siren screaming;

a drunk on a sidewalk
sprays bushes with urine,
sings some unrecognizable melody;

leather-clad rockers hand-in-hand
frequent taco stand next to alley filled
with bums, winos, and the dispossessed;

bent old woman passes by with fumbling steps,
her shopping cart peopled with lost dreams;
check back in a decade or so, we'll all be here.

HARRY MISCONSTRUES BERKELEY

If a man were to hit the floor
in his living room, the old requiescat
in pace routine, if he kicked up
a fuss on the way out, noise, noise,
and more noise, and no witnesses
abounded in the region, nary a one,
did he really die? Did he make
a sound? Does it matter,
alone, alone-o? Chew on that,
all you denizens of Philosophy 101.

Daddy Daddy -- sighed his daughter -- with you
everything is too personal.

Growled Harry, tell it to the citizens
of the boneyard; tell it to the widows
and widowers awaiting their summons;
tell it to dying stars; tell it to nonagenarians
slipping into silence without witness.

She patted his shoulder as she exited
back into her busy world, where all
seemed so certain of existence, where
philosophy had so little to do with life.

Alone in his living room, Harry danced
a slow jig, muttered to himself,
did that actually happen? Do I count as a witness?
If I take a nap unaccompanied, do I exist?

HARRY THE MUSIC CRITIC

"If you're into fine wine, Mozart
is an okay way to pass the time.
                                                  But if you
dig the hard stuff, Muddy
Waters is your man: he'll rearrange
your brain, get your feet
chugging like a freight train;

you might even last the night
without saying her name -- the one
who keeps tilting your elbow from
all those miles and years away.

Sing hey lack a day, let the sun shine in,
and maybe check out Mance Lipscomb
Son House, say hello to Junior Wells,
visit *Money Jungle* and learn how the Duke,

Mingus, and Roach make jazz cook harder than most
blues, and listen to the pain of all these gents
in order to forget your own. Before returning
home, toss back a shot of Bach to smooth out

your memory, the night, your wild desire
to dance up one wall and down the next.
Lift a glass to all those who help your soul
unchain itself and sashay through the world."

HARRY ABANDONED YET AGAIN

casual flip of hand
goodbye without goodbye

more contemptuous than words

leaves me out of breath
or thought

yell curse punch me

these signify engagement
a possibility of hope

casual flip of hand

does not even rise
to level of damnation

FADING HARRY

Friends and family slip away
like leaves on an autumn wind
like snow melting

like towns boarded up
and vanishing in time's waters
and Harry weeps and knows not

for whom or what or why
save perhaps his realization
no one and nothing seems to him

tied to his past or present or whatever future
may loom as he wanders here and there
in a land he no longer recognizes

he gathers a handful of fallen leaves
contemplates them bestows them on the wind

CRANKY HARRY

at end of long, boring day,
wanders abroad through city
side streets, releasing angst
with each step, each exhalation

of breath, each mutter
of casual complaint,
looks up and realizes
day fades, crepuscule lingers

in western sky, last whispers
of day and remaining colors
hang as though the final notes
of a Clark Terry flugelhorn solo

swinging, singing even as they fade
into memory and so the sky above.

HARRY WHO HAS NEVER GROWN UP

Harry, that old reprobate
whose daughter vanished
into undergraduate, then
graduate life, whose wife
is a ghost in a bourbon
bottle and whose lips
intoxicate from decades past,
whose scent enchants
whenever he wanders past
a garden in full bloom, that Harry

lives only in memory these days.
He sees lads kicking a football
or hitting a baseball and can smell
the fields and hear the cries
of boyhood. On a rainy day,
he walks into a forest and prays
the silence will bless him as it did
when he roamed forests alone
as a teenager, and a future,
both real and imagined, will

fill his tired mind once again
with hope, with a willingness
to dare, with the wild imagination
that long ago blessed him before
he destroyed love without awareness
of what he was doing. Old songs,
pictures of a faded past, names
only half-remembered, all fill
him with a sorrow he can neither
control nor justify. He falls asleep

on a couch and his memories drown
slowly in a half-empty glass of whiskey.

SUCH SWEET PARTING SAYS HARRY

her crooked grin
a shard of glass

shaped like a scimitar
carved out my heart

on her way out the door
she juggled her relic

of our years together
all the way down the driveway

then tossed it in a rubbish bin
with a behind the back pass

I will be okay I told myself
as I knocked back half

a bottle of Jack Daniels
and sank into a chair

this will be my life
in the words of an old song

"Oh Whiskey, Rye Whiskey, Whiskey I cried
If I don't get rye Whiskey I surely will die"

Oh Harry, old Harry, you're surely a fool
your life is the life of somebody's tool

slowly I rocked the evening away
lost in meaningless reverie

laughing at myself laughing at life
laughing at the tears waiting to come

HARRY'S PSALM

In the cold vastness of space without end,
we swirl through time, around the sun,
alone, unknown, unknowable, lonely

collections of stardust, certain we matter,
but vague as to why and how, unable
to prove our value, yet convinced we must

matter, that the matter which forms us
is formed around a ghost within the machine
that is each of us, whether alone or together;

and we pray, we bray like jackasses how unique
we each are, we rant, we rave, we demand
recognition, unable to recognize our connection

to everything else in the known and knowable
universe; we are built from the building blocks
that form all else, but would deny the connection,

seeking connection with the unknowable,
the invisible, the unfathomable, while ignoring
the wonder of our connection with all that exists;

from (star)dust we came, to (star)dust we return,
and we are sister and brother to the glorious beauty
of star, black hole, moon, field, forest, mountain, river,

stream, ocean, plant, insect, mammal, reptile, fish,
and amphibian, as well as the sensuous delight of sound --
bird call, waterfall, wolf howl, symphony, jazz combo,

electric guitar, fiddle, bagpipe, mandolin, bouzouki, sax,
and oud, the roar of ocean's arrival at shore, the whisper
and murmur of stream, brook, hushed midnight

rainfall, the exhalation of breath as snow falls,
the magnificence of lightning and the wild power of thunder --
all, all, all is each of us, and each of us is all that surrounds us

and abounds throughout all that can be seen and not seen;
yet even with this extraordinary outpouring of which
we are part, we are, in heart and mind, too often alone

and desperate, unwilling to recognize the all that is
in us and the us that is in all we see and imagine.
And all that is tumbles toward the dust which has

formed us all, and calls us back to be reshaped
again and again until there is no longer any stardust
to conjure wild beauty in the midst of the cold void.

HARRY DEFINES RESURRECTION

After the boredom, the lassitude,
the heat, the retreat to sleep,
a breeze insinuates itself
between the yawn and the stretch,
and will is reborn -- airborne
like certain seeds -- and with it
come desire and the long tangle
of vines from which, dangling
tenaciously, one discovers the jewel
hope, hope, blessed sacramental hope.

BIOGRAPHY

Michael L. Newell was born in Florida in 1945. In addition to living in thirteen states, he has lived in Japan, The Philippine Islands, Thailand, The United Arab Emirates, Jordan, Kuwait, Uzbekistan, Mexico, Egypt, Estonia, Saudi Arabia, Bolivia, and Rwanda. He currently lives in a small town on the Florida coast.

Newell studied writing with Benjamin Saltman and Ann Stanford. His poems have appeared in a number of periodicals including *Aethlon: The Journal of Sport Literature*; *Bellowing Ark*; *College English*; *Current*; *English Journal*; *First Class*; *The Iconoclast*; *Issa's Untidy Hut*; *Jerry Jazz Musician*; *Lilliput Review*; *Poetry Depth Quarterly*; *Rattle*; *Shemom*; *Ship of Fools*; *Tulane Review*; and *Verse-Virtual*.

Some of his previous books include *A Stranger to the Land*; *Seeking Shelter*; *A Long Time Traveling*; *Traveling without Compass or Map*; *Meditation of an Old Man Standing on a Bridge*; *Wandering*; *Each Step a Discovery*; and *Making My Peace*.

COMMENTS ON THIS BOOK

This collection of Michael Newell's Harry poems is something special and long overdue. It is a life-long project that, poem by poem, builds up a complex and distinct persona who endures life's trials and undergoes all sorts of moods. Newell expresses Harry's unique and trenchant sensibility in verses of many forms, in the precise and condensed diction of poetry. Taken together, they achieve the scope of a novel. Harry's sadness is more than cheerless, his bitterness beyond biting, his joy the more jubilant for being hard-won and rare. The collection offers an advanced course in the awareness of the self and the world, lessons in consciousness that are sometimes harsh but unfailingly human and humane.

--Robert Wexelblatt, Author of *Hsi-wei Tales, The Thirteenth Studebaker, Losses*, etc.

Within these pages, Harry lives as a man dearly in love with life, "his fingers burn in remembrance." He is present in walkabouts, taking in the real world, overcome with human frailties, yet "dazed with unutterable hope." He is so downtrodden at times, I find myself wishing he was more than a character in a book so that I could take him in my arms and tell him, "Everything is going to be okay."

—Stellasue Lee, author of *Queen of Jacks, New and Selected Works*.

In Michael L. Newell's *The Harry Poems*, Newell's latest volume of poetry, Newell brings to life Harry a man who is awake to life, attentive to nature, alive to music, and alert to memories that move him. Yet Harry's sensitive attributes also make him vulnerable to the sting and ongoing defeats that fracture him. Different from previous poetry books by Newell, in *The Harry Poems,* Newell focuses on giving voice to the difficult loneliness, griefs, and soundless regrets that howl in the heart's hidden corners and crevices longing to tumble out. Newell deftly brings to life the interplay of beauty and grief in these poems. As Harry says in "Harry the Old Optimist,"

A future will bloom from what I cart inside me:

compost of years -- dreams, fears, triumphs, defeats,
a rich decay from which will arise new
… Beauty, [which] even now can seize me by the throat

In these poems, discover again Newell's ability to reveal life's pulse, even amidst difficulty and despair.

--Anna Citrino, author of *A Space Between*.

In *The Harry Poems*, Michael L. Newell creates a persona so that he can funnel his extraordinary gifts into passages that shift from sensual delight to exuberance to melancholy in the turn of a phrase. Harry gives us moments of intimacy, moments of anguish, moments of irony. Sometimes Harry stands aloof. Sometimes he dances. The language always dances.

--Ed Ruzicka, author of My *Life with Cars* and *Engines of Belief.*

www.ingramcontent.com/pod-product-compliance
Lightning Source LLC
LaVergne TN
LVHW010237200726
843506LV00014B/3013